Know Thyself
Mental Health
Awareness

By

Lisa M Harper

The moral right of the author has been asserted

The Empire Publishers publishing
12808 West Airport Blvd Suite 270M Sugar Land, TX 77478

https://empirepublishers.co/about-us

Our books may be purchased in bulk for promotional,
educational, or business use.
Please contact The Empire Publishers at +(844) 636-4576, or by
email at support@theempirepublishers.com

First Edition September 2024

About the Author

Lisa M Harper is a daughter of the most high God, stepping out in faith to produce a book on mental health. She is creative, adventurous, and determined to bring value and perspective to the book publishing world. She has been empowered by God with an intuitive spirit, using her own experience in her mental health journey and God's word to bring a fresh perspective to mental health. Using the intuitive power of self-awareness, God's word, and the connection to community.

To all who struggle inside, there is hope, don't give up!

Table of Contents

Introduction

Have you ever felt overwhelmed by stress, anxious about the future, or struggled to understand your own emotions? If you have then you're not alone. Millions of people grapple with mental health challenges that can significantly impact their lives. Feeling lost or out of control is scary, but there's hope for a more fulfilling and mentally healthy life.

In a world where holistic well-being is increasingly sought after, this book serves as a guiding light for individuals navigating the complexities of life. Holistic well-being encompasses your emotional, spiritual, and relational health. It's not just about feeling good; it's about thriving in all aspects of your life.

While external factors can play a role, the optimistic news is that we have significant power over our own mental well-being. This book empowers you to take charge of your journey towards mental health by fostering self-awareness.

Self-awareness is the foundation for positive change. By understanding your thoughts, emotions, and behaviors, you'll be better equipped to navigate life's challenges. This book will guide you through this process, providing practical tools and exercises to cultivate self-knowledge.

But self-awareness alone isn't enough. We are social creatures who thrive in connection. This book emphasizes the importance of building a supportive community. Isolation can exacerbate mental health struggles, while strong relationships provide a vital safety net. Here, you'll discover how to build and nurture these connections, fostering a sense of belonging and acceptance.

Crucially, you'll also explore the role of faith. The Bible offers a wealth of wisdom and comfort for those struggling with mental health. You'll learn that God understands your struggles and desires a relationship with you, even in your darkest moments. This book will help you cultivate a deeper connection with God, finding solace and strength in your faith.

By referring to the Bible, this book will also shed light on the concept of mindfulness through allusions and stories. Take King David in Psalms 46:10: 'Be still, and know that I am God.' This verse encourages quiet reflection, a core principle of mindfulness, which can help us confront anxieties. By acknowledging God's presence (and sovereignty in our circumstances) and calming our minds, we gain a clearer perspective to navigate away from the darkness that can consume us.

The story of David and Jonathan exemplifies the power of a deep and supportive friendship, reminding us that we were not meant to walk this journey alone.

The Bible also offers practical tools to cultivate inner peace. Prayer becomes a direct line to a source of strength greater than ourselves. Meditation, practiced by figures like David in the Psalms, allows us to quiet the constant mental chatter and connect with something deeper. Finally, a dash of old-fashioned soul-searching, like the introspection wrestled with by Paul in his letters, can unearth a reservoir of resilience we never knew we possessed. Through these practices, the Bible doesn't promise a quick fix but a path to lasting strength and inner peace.

The question is: What is mental health?

According to the CDC definition, 'Mental health includes our emotional, psychological, and social well-being. It affects how we think, feel, and act. It also helps determine how we handle stress, relate to others, and make healthy choices."

Life's stressors, transitions, and challenges can impact mental health at any stage of life. By promoting awareness and understanding of mental health issues in workplaces, communities, and families, we encourage individuals to prioritize their mental well-being and seek help when needed.

Mental health awareness is crucial because it breaks down the stigma surrounding mental illness. By openly discussing mental health, we challenge misconceptions and encourage people to seek help without fear of judgement. This not only benefits those struggling themselves but also allows friends, family, and caregivers to better understand and support them. Ultimately, increased awareness paves the way for improved mental health resources and care for everyone.

There are many misconceptions prevalent about mental health. One such is the belief that mental health issues are a sign of weakness or personal failure. In reality, mental health conditions are complex and multifaceted, often stemming from a combination of genetic, biological, environmental, and psychological factors. Just as individuals can experience physical ailments, such as diabetes or heart disease, without it reflecting on their character or worth, mental health conditions are not indicative of personal weakness or deficiency. Another misconception is that mental health problems are rare or uncommon.

In truth, mental health issues are prevalent worldwide, affecting individuals of all ages, backgrounds, and walks of life. According to the World Health Organization, approximately one in four people will experience a mental health disorder at some point in their lives. However, due to stigma and fear of judgment, many individuals may hesitate to seek help, leading to underreporting and a lack of awareness about the true prevalence of mental health issues.

Furthermore, there is a misconception that mental health conditions are permanent and untreatable. While some mental health disorders may require long-term management and support, many are treatable with appropriate interventions, including therapy, medication, lifestyle changes, and social support. The stigma surrounding mental health can also lead to the misconception that discussing or seeking help for mental health concerns is taboo or unnecessary.

In reality, open and honest conversations about mental health are essential for reducing *misunderstandings,* promoting awareness, and encouraging individuals to seek support. By creating safe spaces for dialogue and providing access to resources and support services, we can empower individuals to prioritize their mental well-being and seek help when needed. Finally, there is a misconception that mental health is separate from physical health when, in fact, the two are closely interconnected.

Isolation, the belief that "God doesn't understand," and the notion of self-reliance are common themes that many individuals grappling with mental health challenges may encounter. These sentiments can create barriers to seeking support and hinder the journey towards healing and well-being. Isolation, whether self-imposed or a result of external circumstances, can intensify feelings of loneliness, despair, and disconnection. It may lead individuals to withdraw from social interactions, further exacerbating their sense of isolation and alienation. Despite the prevalence of social media and digital connectivity, many individuals still experience profound feelings of loneliness and isolation, which can have detrimental effects on their mental health.

The belief that "God doesn't understand" adds another layer to these's challenges. Individuals may feel disconnected from their faith or spiritual beliefs, believing that their struggles are incompatible with God's understanding or support. This perception can lead to feelings of alienation from religious or spiritual communities and a sense of spiritual distress. Additionally, the notion of self-reliance can be both a coping mechanism and a hindrance to seeking help for mental health issues. While independence and self-sufficiency are admirable traits, they can also prevent individuals from reaching out for support when needed. The misconception that one should be able to handle one's struggles alone may prevent individuals from seeking professional help or leaning on their support networks for assistance. Recognizing and addressing these barriers is essential for individuals to receive the support they need to navigate their mental health challenges and work towards healing and recovery.

For me and many others, these barriers to seeking support for mental health challenges have been significant hurdles on the path to healing.

There have been times when I've felt isolated, believing that no one could possibly understand what I was going through. I've grappled with the misconception that I should be able to handle my struggles on my own without burdening others or seeking external help. And there have been moments when I've questioned whether my faith and spirituality were compatible with my mental health journey, leading to feelings of confusion and doubt. However, I've also learned that reaching out for support is not a sign of weakness but a courageous act of self-care.

Opening up to trusted friends, family members, or mental health professionals has allowed me to break free from the shackles of isolation and self-reliance, finding solace and support in the midst of my struggles. And I've discovered that my faith and spirituality can be sources of strength and comfort, guiding me through the darkest moments and reminding me that I am never alone.

So, this book isn't a one-stop shop for mental health but a supportive guide on your path to holistic well-being. It equips you with tools for self-awareness, creates connections that replace isolation with the warmth of community, and explores the Bible's timeless wisdom for comfort and strength.

Here, you'll discover, as Maya Angelou so eloquently phrased it, "Still I Rise," for healing and wholeness are within reach.

Remember, the journey of a thousand miles begins with a single step.

Are you ready to take that first step?

Chapter 1:
Why Mental Health Matters

The mind is everything. What you think you become.

–Buddha

In today's fast-paced world, how often do we stop to consider the well-being of our own minds? Mental health is an essential yet often overlooked aspect of our overall well-being. It impacts how we perceive ourselves, navigate daily life, connect with God, and build meaningful relationships with others.

Many of you might have felt like you were drowning in a sea of worries. Perhaps your thoughts race uncontrollably, leaving you feeling overwhelmed and anxious. Maybe you struggle with low moods, a lack of motivation, or difficulty connecting with others.

There's no doubt that mental health, the state of our emotional, psychological, and social well-being, is often a neglected aspect of overall health. Statistics tell a concerning picture:

According to the National Institute of Mental Health (NIMH), in the United States alone, one in five adults experiences a mental illness in a given year.

The World Health Organization (WHO) reports that one in ten people globally suffers from a mental disorder.

Mental health conditions are the leading cause of disability worldwide, with depression alone accounting for over 328 million cases globally, according to WHO.

These numbers highlight the alarming prevalence of mental health issues in our society. But why is mental health so important? Why should we prioritize it alongside physical well-being? The answer lies in the relation of mind and body.

When our mental health suffers, it can manifest in various ways, impacting not only our thoughts and emotions but also our physical well-being. For example, anxiety can lead to physical symptoms like headaches, stomachaches, and fatigue. Depression can manifest in changes in sleep patterns, appetite, and energy levels.

Conversely, neglecting our physical health can also negatively impact our mental well-being. Poor sleep habits, unhealthy eating patterns, and lack of exercise have all been linked to increased anxiety, depression, and other mental health challenges. This mind-body connection emphasizes the importance of a holistic approach to well-being, where we prioritize both physical and mental health for optimal functioning.

How Mental Health Impacts Daily Life

The impact of mental health transcends the realm of statistics and medical journals. It's way bigger than that. It's the invisible hand shaping our everyday lives - how we see ourselves, our connection with something bigger, whether that's God, the universe, and how we treat the people around us. If we leave mental health issues untreated, it can have a significant cascading effect, impacting various aspects of our lives. When an untreated crack in a foundation is ignored, it will weaken a building. Likewise, unaddressed mental health issues can erode our sense of well-being, our relationships, and even our connection with God.

Seeing Ourselves Clearly Through the Lens of Self

When issues related to mental health remain unaddressed, our self-perception gets affected. When anxiety and negativity surround our minds, we tend to view ourselves through a harsh and critical lens. Studies by the American Psychological Association (APA) reveal a strong correlation between mental health conditions and low self-esteem. Individuals struggling with depression often experience feelings of worthlessness and hopelessness.

This distorted self-image can be a significant barrier to personal growth and fulfillment. Philosopher and psychologist Carl Jung emphasized the importance of self-awareness, stating, "Knowing your own darkness is the best method for dealing with the darkness of other people." When we prioritize our mental well-being, we can create a clearer understanding of ourselves, our strengths, and our weaknesses. This self-awareness allows us to replace negative self-talk with compassion and acceptance, promoting a more positive and realistic self-image.

However, when mental health struggles go unchecked, they can significantly impact our self-perception. Constant anxiety can make us feel perpetually on edge and unsafe. Depression can lead to feelings of worthlessness and hopelessness. Untreated mental health issues can make it difficult to connect with others and contribute meaningfully, further reinforcing negative self-perceptions. In such times, philosopher and psychologist Alfred Adler emphasize the importance of developing a sense of belonging and contributing to society.

Mental Health and Relationships

Mental health doesn't just affect us internally; it significantly impacts how we connect with others. Just as a strong foundation is essential for a sturdy building, healthy mental well-being forms the bedrock for strong and meaningful relationships. When our mental health suffers, we might struggle to connect with others on a deeper level. Social anxiety, for example, can make it difficult to initiate conversations or participate in social gatherings. Depression can manifest in withdrawal and a lack of interest in spending time with loved ones.

A study published in the "Journal of Personality and Social Psychology" found that individuals with depression are more likely to experience relationship problems. This lack of connection can be isolating and worsen feelings of loneliness and hopelessness, creating a vicious cycle. On the other hand, when our mental health is in check, we're better equipped to build and maintain healthy relationships. We can be more present, empathetic, and patient with others. We can communicate effectively and build trust, nurturing a sense of connection and belonging.

The Spiritual Connection: Mental Health and Our Relationship with God

Our mental well-being also plays a crucial role in shaping our connection with God. When anxiety and negativity cloud our minds, it can be difficult to experience the peace, hope, and joy God offers. We might struggle to pray, feel distant from God's presence, or even question His love for us.

The Bible is filled with stories of individuals who wrestled with mental health challenges. *In the book of Psalms*, King David writes extensively about his struggles with depression, crying out in Psalm 42:9, "Why hast thou forgotten me? Why dost thou make me go about in mourning because of the enemy?" David's raw honesty reminds us that even those close to God can experience emotional turmoil.

In my experience, mental struggles have connected me closer to God. For it is in my darkest moments that I cry out to Him for help, and He always meets me there. I have struggled with anxiety to the point where I eventually needed medication. It took years before I realized this, and the only thing that got me through was asking God for help, one moment at a time. You do not need to be mentally healthy to connect with God; you just need to seek Him (Matthew 6:31-34) and know Him for who He is. His word is a love story biography of who He is.

However, ignoring these struggles can impact a relationship with God, making it harder to see His love and grace. Author and pastor Rick Warren reminds us, "A healthy soul is the playground of the Holy Spirit." Through the power of faith in our Creator, we can overcome many mental barriers and experience a deeper transformation as whole individuals.

The Link Between Mental and Physical Health

The human body is a magnificent system, with each organ and system playing a vital role in the harmony of life. Mental health, far from being a separate entity, is woven into physical well-being. Just as a well-tuned instrument contributes to a melodious melody, good mental health contributes to a healthy body.

Food and Mental Well-being

The old adage "you are what you eat" holds significant weight when considering the link between mental and physical health. The food we choose to fuel our bodies directly impacts our brain function and emotional state. Studies published in the journal "Nutritional Neuroscience" have found a strong connection between a healthy diet rich in fruits, vegetables, and whole grains and improved mood and cognitive function.

Equally, a diet high in processed foods, sugar, and unhealthy fats has been linked to an increased risk of depression and anxiety. This is because these foods can disrupt the delicate balance of neurotransmitters in the brain, chemicals that regulate mood, sleep, and cognitive function. It is like when a car runs poorly on low-quality fuel, our brains struggle to function optimally when we don't nourish them with the right nutrients.

The Power of Exercise

Physical activity isn't just about building muscle or achieving a certain body type; it's a powerful tool for promoting mental well-being. Exercise releases endorphins, natural mood elevators that combat stress and anxiety. A study published in the journal "Depression and Anxiety" found that regular exercise can be as effective as medication in treating mild to moderate depression.

Physical activity also improves sleep quality, which is crucial for mental health. When we're sleep-deprived, our brains struggle to regulate emotions, focus, and make sound decisions. On the contrary, good sleep habits contribute to feelings of calmness, clarity, and improved emotional resilience.

Self-Perception and Physical Health

Our self-image, significantly influenced by mental health, also plays a role in our physical well-being. Individuals struggling with negative body image might be more likely to engage in unhealthy eating habits or neglect exercise due to feelings of shame or inadequacy. This can lead to weight fluctuations, malnutrition, and an increased risk of chronic diseases.

Similarly, a positive body image, fostered by healthy self-esteem and mental well-being, can motivate us to make healthy choices that nourish our bodies. We're more likely to engage in activities that make us feel good, both physically and mentally, creating a positive feedback loop that benefits our overall health.

Finding Hope in the Bible

While the Bible doesn't use the modern term "mental health," it speaks extensively about our emotional well-being and God's compassion for those who struggle. Throughout the Bible, we find encouragement, guidance, and examples of individuals who grappled with mental health challenges:

- **King David:** A man after God's own heart, David wrote extensively about his struggles with depression in the Psalms. In Psalm 42, he cries out, "As the deer pants for streams of water, so my soul pants for you, O God." David's raw honesty in the Psalms reminds us that even the faithful experience emotional distress, and God desires us to bring our burdens to Him.

- **Elijah:** A courageous prophet, Elijah felt overwhelmed and discouraged to the point of wishing for death (1 Kings 19:4). This story shows us that even strong figures in the Bible faced mental health challenges. It also highlights God's care, as He provided Elijah with rest, food, and reassurance (1 Kings 19:5-8).

- **Job:** Job endured immense suffering and loss, questioning God's presence and purpose in his life. The Book of Job offers a powerful reminder that God remains faithful even in the midst of our deepest struggles.

These stories not only offer comfort but also highlight God's firm love and care for his children. When Elijah felt discouraged, God provided him with rest and reassurance (1 Kings 19:5-8). Similarly, when David felt overwhelmed, he turned to God in prayer and worship, finding solace and strength (Psalm 38).

The Bible is filled with verses that remind us of God's compassion and presence during challenging times. Philippians 4:6-7 encourages us, "Do not be anxious about anything, but in every situation, by prayer and petition, with thanksgiving, present your requests to God. And the peace of God, which transcends all understanding, will guard your hearts and your minds in Christ Jesus." This verse emphasizes the power of prayer and trusting God to bring peace even amidst anxiety.

What Are We Supposed to Do?

The Bible encourages us to love our neighbors as we love ourselves (Matthew 22:39), Which includes taking care of our mental health and seeking help when needed. Just as we wouldn't hesitate to seek medical attention for a physical illness, we shouldn't be ashamed to seek help for mental health challenges.

Proverbs 18:15 advises, "The heart of the discerning acquires knowledge, for the ears of the wise seek knowledge." Seeking professional help, spiritual guidance, or knowledge about mental health can be a way of honoring God's gift of wisdom and taking responsibility for our well-being.

God Cares About Mental Health and Others

The Bible also emphasizes our responsibility towards one another. Leviticus 25:35 instructs, "If any of your fellow Israelites become poor and unable to support themselves among their fellow Israelites, you are to help them up, whether a foreigner or someone who lives among you." This verse, while referring to physical poverty, can be applied to the concept of mental well-being. We can create a community of care that reflects God's love for all His children by offering a listening ear, encouraging professional help, and showing compassion.

Chapter 2
Types of Mental Health Disorders

"Come to me, all who labor and are heavily laden, and I will give you rest. Take my yoke upon you, and learn from me, for I am gentle and lowly in heart, and you will find rest for your souls."

- Matthew 11:28-29

These words, spoken by Jesus, offer a promise of solace and peace. Yet, in today's fast-paced and often overwhelming world, many find themselves struggling to find that inner peace. Look around you - a colleague seems perpetually stressed, a friend withdraws from social gatherings, and a loved one battles negative self-talk. These are just a few examples of the growing prevalence of mental health challenges in our society.

The causes of these mental health struggles are many-sided. Factors like social media pressures, economic uncertainty, and a culture of constant comparison can contribute to feelings of anxiety, isolation, and inadequacy. Furthermore, the COVID-19 pandemic has exacerbated these challenges, leading to increased stress, loneliness, and social isolation.

In light of these realities, understanding common mental health disorders becomes crucial. By becoming familiar with the signs and symptoms of these conditions, we can better equip ourselves to handle our own mental well-being and offer support to those who might be struggling. This chapter will explore some of the most common mental health disorders, including:

- Depression

- Anxiety disorders

- Panic disorder

- Eating disorders

- Social anxiety disorder

- Addictive behaviors

This chapter will look into each of these conditions, exploring their characteristics and how they manifest in our thoughts, emotions, and behaviors.

Biblical Wisdom and Mental Health

The Bible, though written centuries ago, offers Insightful wisdom that can illiterate mental health struggles in ourselves and others. While it doesn't use modern medical terminology, it comprehensively employs influencing imagery to explain the challenges we might face. Let's explore some Biblical principles that can help us recognize signs of mental health issues:

- **Changes in Mood and Behavior:** 1 Samuel 16:14 But the Spirit of the Lord departed form Saul, and a distressing spirit form the Lord troubled him. After the Spirit of the Lord left Saul, his mood and behavior changed drastically. He became distressed, paranoid, and was often overwhelmed with a troubling spirit, leading to erratic behavior. This change in mood eventually led to his increasing jealousy and hostility.

- **Changes in Sleep Patterns:** In Genesis, after God formed His creation, he rested. This emphasizes the importance of healthy sleep patterns. Difficulty falling asleep, staying asleep, or sleeping excessively can be signs of underlying emotional distress.

- **Changes in Appetite:** Proverbs 23:20-21 warns against those who "feast continually...for such people come to poverty and wear tattered clothes." This verse highlights the potential for unhealthy eating habits to be a coping mechanism for emotional struggles. Significant changes in appetite, either loss of interest in food or overeating, can be a sign of a mental health disorder.

- **Withdrawal from Social Activities:** Proverbs 18:1 reads, "Whoever isolates himself seeks his own desire; he breaks out against all sound judgment." This verse suggests that social isolation can be a symptom of deeper emotional turmoil. Someone who withdraws from social activities they once enjoyed or avoids spending time with loved ones might be struggling with a mental health challenge.

- **Difficulty Concentrating or Making Decisions:** Proverbs 12:25 states, "Anxiety in a man's heart weighs him down, but a good word makes him glad." This verse connects emotional distress with difficulty focusing and making clear decisions. Feeling overwhelmed, forgetful, or struggling to concentrate on tasks can be signs of anxiety or depression.

These are just general signs, and the specific symptoms can vary depending on the individual and the disorder. However, by keeping these principles in mind and drawing wisdom from the Bible, we can become more attuned to potential mental health struggles in ourselves and those around us.

1. Depression

Depression, a thief of joy and motivation, is a common foe. Defined by the National Institute of Mental Health as a serious medical illness impacting mood, thought patterns, and daily life, depression goes far beyond a temporary bout of sadness. It lingers a persistent weight that can last for weeks, months, or even years.

Myths vs. Facts:

One pervasive myth surrounding depression is that it's simply a matter of feeling down for a short while. In reality, depression is a distinct condition characterized by a profound sense of hopelessness and a loss of interest in activities once enjoyed. Imagine someone who used to find solace in painting but now struggles to pick up a brush. Another misconception is that depression indicates weakness. However, it's a medical illness, and just like any other illness, it can affect anyone regardless of personality or strength. Biological factors, life experiences, and even genetics can all play a role.

What does this look like in behaviors?

The outward signs of depression can manifest in various ways. Social withdrawal is a common symptom. An individual who previously thrived in social settings might now isolate themselves, avoiding gatherings and spending less time with loved ones. Personal hygiene tasks like showering or maintaining a clean living space can become overwhelming burdens. Sleep and appetite can also be disrupted, with difficulty falling asleep, early morning awakenings, or significant changes in eating habits becoming a regular occurrence.

Moreover, concentration and decision-making can also suffer. Someone struggling with depression might find it hard to focus on tasks, feeling forgetful and easily distracted. Increased irritability or sudden anger outbursts can also be a sign of the emotional turmoil brewing beneath the surface.

What does it feel like?

The internal experience of depression is often characterized by a pervasive sense of negativity. Feelings of sadness, hopelessness, and worthlessness become constant companions. A dark cloud seems to loom, casting a shadow over everything. Activities that once brought joy, like spending time with friends or pursuing hobbies, lose their appeal. The ability to experience positive emotions can be significantly diminished, leaving a sense of emotional numbness. Fatigue and a lack of energy can make even the simplest tasks feel insurmountable. In severe cases, individuals might grapple with intrusive thoughts of death or suicide.

What does the Bible say about this? Who in the bible struggled with this?

The Bible offers a relatable perspective on mental health struggles. Psalms, a collection of poems and prayers, are filled with expressions of emotional turmoil. In Psalm 42:6, the Psalmist cries out, "Why are you downcast, O my soul? Why are you disquieted within me?" These raw words paint a vivid image of emotional distress. Similarly, the story of Jonah portrays a prophet who becomes overwhelmed by his calling and flees from God. Jonah's experience reflects the feelings of anxiety and despair that can accompany depression. These examples serve as a powerful reminder that even those with a deep faith can struggle with emotional challenges.

2. Anxiety disorder

Unlike heavy depression, anxiety disorders manifest as a constant state of worry and unease. It can be defined as a group of mental illnesses, anxiety disorders cause excessive and persistent worry that significantly impacts daily life. It's important to differentiate between occasional anxiety, a normal human response to stress, and an anxiety disorder, which is characterized by a pervasive and debilitating level of worry.

Debunking Common Misconceptions

One common misconception surrounding anxiety disorders is that they're simply a case of being uptight or nervous. However, the reality is far more complex. Anxiety disorders are not a sign of weakness but rather a medical condition that can be effectively treated. Another myth suggests there's nothing you can do about anxiety. Fortunately, therapy, medication, or a combination of both can significantly improve the quality of life for those struggling with anxiety disorders.

Recognizing the Signs

The outward signs of anxiety disorders can vary depending on the specific type of disorder. However, some general behavioral changes might be observed. Restlessness is a common symptom, with individuals feeling like they can't relax or sit still. Difficulty concentrating and making decisions can also be a challenge. Physical symptoms like muscle tension, headaches, and fatigue are also frequently reported. In some cases, avoidance behaviors become a coping mechanism. Someone with social anxiety, for instance, might avoid social situations altogether to prevent the anxiety they trigger.

What Anxiety Feels Like

The internal experience of anxiety is often characterized by a persistent feeling of being on edge. Excessive worry about everyday situations, both big and small, becomes a constant companion. The mind might race with worst-case scenarios, fueling the feeling of impending doom. Physical symptoms like a racing heart, shortness of breath, and dizziness can exacerbate the sense of panic and unease. Relaxation becomes difficult, and the ability to feel calm feels like a distant memory.

Faith and Anxiety

The Bible acknowledges the human experience of anxiety. In Philippians 4:6, the Apostle Paul instructs us, "Do not be anxious about anything, but in every situation, by prayer and petition, with thanksgiving, present your requests to God." This verse, while encouraging trust in God, acknowledges the reality of anxiety. The story of Moses in Exodus 4 also offers a glimpse into anxiety. When confronted with the task of leading the Israelites out of Egypt, Moses expresses doubt and anxiety, stating, "I am not eloquent, neither have I been in the past or since you began to speak to me. I am slow of speech and of tongue" (Exodus 4:10). Moses' experience resonates with the feelings of inadequacy and self-doubt that can accompany anxiety. These examples highlight that even figures of faith can grapple with anxiety, and there is no shame in seeking help for this condition.

3. Panic Disorder

Panic disorder, unlike the constant worry of generalized anxiety, is characterized by sudden and unexpected panic attacks. Commonly defined as a type of anxiety disorder, these attacks can be terrifying and debilitating, often occurring without any warning. It is like feeling perfectly fine one moment and then being struck with a wave of intense fear the next.

Separating Fact from Fiction

One myth surrounding panic disorder is that it's simply a case of overreacting to a situation. However, panic attacks are intense physiological responses that feel very real and can be incredibly frightening. Another misconception is that experiencing a single panic attack means you have a panic disorder. Panic disorder is diagnosed when these attacks become recurrent and significantly impact daily life.

What are its Symptoms?

The outward signs of panic disorder are most evident during a panic attack. Physical symptoms like a racing heart, shortness of breath, chest pain, dizziness, or sweating can come on suddenly and intensely. Feeling like you're choking or having a heart attack is a common experience during a panic attack. Behavioral changes might also be observed, such as a fear of being in places where escape might be difficult or a constant need to be near a trusted friend or family member for reassurance. In severe cases, individuals might restrict their activities significantly to avoid situations that trigger panic attacks.

What does it feel like?

The internal experience of a panic attack is often described as a feeling of intense fear and a sense of losing control. The physical symptoms can be so overwhelming that they fuel the fear, creating a vicious cycle. Thoughts might race with catastrophic scenarios, further intensifying the anxiety. Feeling detached from reality or like you're outside your own body (depersonalization) can also occur. The overwhelming feeling of panic can make it difficult to think clearly or reason effectively.

Finding Answers in the Bible

The Bible offers stories that resonate with the experience of intense fear and anxiety. In 1 Kings 19:3-4, we see Elijah, the prophet, fleeing from Queen Jezebel after a dramatic showdown. The text describes him as "afraid" and requesting death, stating, "I have had enough, Lord. Take my life..." Elijah's experience, while not a clinical diagnosis of panic disorder, portrays the paralyzing fear and sense of being overwhelmed that can accompany such an episode. These examples serve as a reminder that even strong individuals can experience moments of intense fear and anxiety.

4. Eating Disorders

Eating disorders aren't simply about a desire to lose weight. They are complex mental health conditions characterized by unhealthy eating habits and a distorted body image. WHO defines them as serious conditions that can affect your emotional and physical health. Unlike occasional dieting or body dissatisfaction, eating disorders involve persistent and unhealthy behaviors that significantly impact daily life.

Myths Demystified

One common myth surrounding eating disorders is that they only affect teenagers or young women. In reality, eating disorders can develop at any age and affect people of all genders and backgrounds. Another misconception is that eating disorders are a conscious choice or a sign of vanity. However, they are complex mental illnesses with underlying emotional and psychological causes.

Behavioral Signs

The outward signs of eating disorders can vary depending on the specific type of disorder (anorexia nervosa, bulimia nervosa, binge-eating disorder, etc.). However, some general behavioral changes might be observed. Restriction of food intake, often to the point of malnutrition, is a common symptom of anorexia nervosa. Bulimia nervosa might manifest through cycles of binge eating followed by purging behaviors like vomiting or laxative abuse. Binge-eating disorder can involve frequent episodes of consuming large amounts of food in a short period, followed by feelings of shame or guilt. In all cases, a preoccupation with food, weight, and body image becomes a dominant feature of daily life.

What does it feel like?

The internal experience of someone with an eating disorder is often characterized by a distorted body image. Despite being thin, someone with anorexia might see themselves as overweight. A persistent fear of weight gain and a relentless pursuit of thinness can consume their thoughts. Feelings of shame, guilt, and anxiety are often present, further fueling unhealthy eating behaviors. In some cases, there might be a sense of control derived from restricting food intake or purging behaviors. However, this control is often fleeting, replaced by a cycle of negative emotions and unhealthy habits.

What does the Bible say about this?

The Bible, while not directly addressing eating disorders, offers principles that promote a healthy body image and self-acceptance. In Genesis 1:27, it states, "So God created mankind in his own image, in the image of God he created them; male and female he created them." This verse emphasizes the inherent value and dignity of every human being, regardless of physical appearance. The story of Sarah, struggling with infertility in Genesis 16, portrays the emotional distress that can accompany societal pressures related to appearance and physical capabilities. These examples highlight the importance of self-worth rooted in identity as a creation of God rather than external measures like weight or appearance.

5. Social Anxiety Disorder

Social anxiety disorder isn't simply shyness. While shyness might involve a preference for solitude, social anxiety disorder is a crippling fear of social situations that can significantly impact daily life. Defined by the National Institute of Mental Health (NIMH) as a mental health condition, it's characterized by an intense fear of being scrutinized, judged, or humiliated by others. Imagine the constant worry of saying something embarrassing or appearing awkward in a social setting.

Misconceptions and Reality

One myth surrounding social anxiety disorder is that it's simply a matter of being introverted. Introverts enjoy solitude and recharge their energy by spending time alone. However, people with social anxiety disorder fear social situations to the point of avoiding them altogether. Another misconception is that social anxiety only affects public speaking. While public speaking anxiety is a common symptom, social anxiety can manifest in any situation involving social interaction, from small gatherings to work meetings.

Signs of Social Anxiety

The outward signs of social anxiety disorder can vary depending on the severity of the condition. Avoidance is a common coping mechanism. Someone with social anxiety might avoid parties, work events, or even going to the grocery store for fear of social interaction. Physical symptoms like blushing, sweating, trembling, or nausea can also occur in social situations. Difficulty making eye contact, speaking in a soft voice, or appearing withdrawn are other behavioral signs. In severe cases, individuals might experience panic attacks triggered by social situations.

What does it feel like?

The internal experience of someone with a social anxiety disorder is often characterized by a pervasive fear of judgment and scrutiny. The mind might race with negative thoughts, imagining all the ways things could go wrong in a social setting. A constant feeling of being watched or evaluated by others can be overwhelming. Shame and embarrassment are common emotions, further fueling the fear of social interaction. The desire for connection and belonging can be strong, yet the fear of rejection can be paralyzing.

The Bible and Social Anxiety

The Bible, while not using modern terminology, offers stories that resonate with the experience of social anxiety. Moses, in Exodus 4:10, expresses self-doubt and anxiety when confronted with the task of leading the Israelites out of Egypt. He tells God, "I am not eloquent, neither have I been in the past or since you began to speak to me. I am slow of speech and of tongue" (Exodus 4:10). Moses' fear of public speaking and feelings of inadequacy mirror the anxieties experienced by many with social anxiety disorder. These examples serve as a reminder that even figures of faith can struggle with social anxieties, and there's no shame in seeking help to manage them.

6. Addictive Behaviors

Addictive behaviors are more than just enjoying something a little too much. They are a complex set of conditions characterized by the uncontrollable urge to engage in a behavior, regardless of the negative consequences. Experts define addiction as a chronic brain disease that disrupts the brain's reward system, motivation, memory, and learning. Simply put, addiction hijacks the brain, making it difficult to resist the urge to engage in addictive behavior, even when it causes harm.

Myths vs. Facts

Unlike the common misconception that addiction is limited to substances like drugs and alcohol, addictive behaviors encompass a wider range of compulsive actions. While substance abuse is a well-known form of addiction, anything that triggers the brain's reward system and leads to uncontrollable behavior can become addictive. This includes activities like gambling, shopping sprees, video games, or even pornography. Another myth suggests that people with addictions simply lack willpower. However, addiction is a disease, not a moral failing. Changes in the brain caused by addiction make it incredibly difficult to resist the urge to engage in the behavior, even when the consequences are negative. The inability to control these urges highlights the disease aspect of addiction, dispelling the myth that willpower alone is enough to overcome it.

What does this look like in behaviors?

The outward signs of addictive behaviors can vary depending on the specific addiction. However, some general patterns might be observed. Preoccupation with addictive behavior and neglecting responsibilities like work, school, or family is a common sign. Lying or manipulating situations to obtain the object of addiction is another red flag. Increased tolerance, meaning needing more and more of the substance or activity to achieve the desired effect, can also occur. Withdrawal symptoms, such as irritability, anxiety, or depression, might manifest when the addictive behavior is stopped. Financial problems or legal issues can also be consequences of uncontrolled addictive behaviors.

What does it feel like?

The internal experience of addiction is often characterized by a powerful craving or urge that feels difficult to resist. The brain prioritizes addictive behavior above all else, leading to a sense of compulsion. Negative emotions like anxiety, boredom, or loneliness might be triggers for the addictive behavior, offering a temporary escape. Shame, guilt, and regret can follow after engaging in the addictive behavior, yet the cycle often repeats. Feelings of loss of control and hopelessness can be overwhelming.

The Bible on Addiction: Hope for Change

The Bible offers principles relevant to overcoming addictive behaviors. In 1 Corinthians 6:12, Paul instructs, "'I have the right to do anything,' you say—but not everything is beneficial. 'I have the right to do anything'—but I will not be mastered by anything." This verse emphasizes the importance of self-control and avoiding behaviors that enslave us. The story of the Prodigal Son in Luke 15 portrays the destructive nature of compulsive behavior and the possibility of redemption through repentance and seeking help. These examples highlight that freedom from addiction is possible and that seeking help is a sign of strength, not weakness.

As the old saying goes, "A healthy mind is a healthy body." Mental health is just as crucial to our overall well-being as physical health. Just as we wouldn't ignore a broken arm, we shouldn't ignore the cracks that can develop in our mental well-being.

This chapter shed light on common mental health disorders. We've explored the emotional terrain of depression, the anxieties that can leave us feeling on edge, and the distorted cases of eating disorders. We've even looked at the Bible, finding not only stories of struggle but also principles of hope and self-worth.

But here's the key takeaway: While we've explored these challenges, mental health isn't just about understanding these struggles. It's about finding the path towards healing. It's about recognizing the signs within ourselves and those around us, the voices of anxiety or the heavy weight of depression. Just like the Psalmist who cried out, "Why are you downcast, O my soul?" (Psalm 42:6), we can acknowledge our struggles.

Remember, you are not alone in this struggle. Help is available, and there is no shame in seeking it. The Bible encourages us to bear one another's burdens (Galatians 6:2). Whether it's through professional help, the support of loved ones, or the solace found in the Bible, there is a path forward. Take that first step. You are stronger than you think, and with courage and compassion, you can find your way back to a place of peace and wholeness.

Chapter 3
Supporting Others and Creating a Supportive Environment

"We are all broken, that's how the light gets in."

- Ernest Hemingway

You might have noticed one of your friends going through a tough time, withdrawing from social activities and overwhelmed by sadness. You might suspect they're struggling with mental health, but how do you offer support? Silence and stigma can be powerful barriers.

This chapter equips you to be a beacon of support. We'll explore how to start open conversations about mental health, address the stigma often associated with it, and build a support network for loved ones on their journey towards healing. By learning to actively listen, encourage professional help when needed, and create a safe space for open communication, we can embody the spirit of Galatians 6:2: "Bear one another's burdens, and so fulfill the law of Christ." Let's start understanding how to bridge the gap between silence and support.

Breaking Down the Walls

Mental health struggles can feel isolating, shrouded in secrecy and misunderstanding. But the first step towards healing, both for ourselves and those we care about is creating open and honest conversations about mental health.

Why Open Conversations Matter:

- **Reduces Stigma:** Talking openly about mental health challenges normalizes them and chips away at the stigma that can prevent people from seeking help. When we create a space where these conversations are commonplace, individuals are less likely to feel ashamed or alone.

- **Promotes Early Intervention:** Open communication allows individuals to express their struggles sooner, enabling them to access support and treatment before their condition worsens. Early intervention can significantly improve treatment outcomes and overall well-being.

- **Strengthens Relationships:** When we confide in loved ones about our mental health struggles, it fosters deeper connections and trust. Feeling understood and supported by those we care about can be a powerful source of strength during challenging times.

Approaching the Conversation:

- **Choose the right time and place:** Find a private, quiet space where you can have a conversation without distractions or interruptions. Look for non-verbal cues that your friend or loved one seems open to talking – relaxed posture, eye contact, willingness to engage in conversation.

- **Start with empathy:** Let the person know you care about them and have noticed they haven't seemed themselves lately. Avoid accusatory language or judgmental statements.

- **Use "I" statements:** Instead of saying, "You seem down lately," try something like, "I've noticed you haven't been participating in activities you usually enjoy. Is everything alright?"

- **Be an active listener:** Give the person your full attention, make eye contact, and avoid interrupting. Ask open-ended questions that encourage them to elaborate on their feelings and experiences.

- **Validate their feelings:** Let them know their feelings are valid, and you understand how difficult things might be for them. Avoid minimizing their struggles or offering unsolicited advice.

- **Focus on listening, not fixing:** Your primary role in this conversation is to offer a safe space for them to express themselves. Resist the urge to offer solutions prematurely.

What to Say and What Not to Say:

- **What to Say:**

    - "I'm here for you, no matter what."

    - "Would you like to talk about what's going on?"

    - "I care about you and your well-being."

    - "Is there anything I can do to help?"

    - "You're not alone in this. Many people struggle with mental health."

- **What Not to Say:**

- "Just get over it." (Minimizes their struggles)

- "Everyone feels that way sometimes." (Invalidates their experience)

- "At least you have it better than others." (Doesn't address their specific needs)

- "You just need to..." (Offers unsolicited advice before listening)

But you must also:

- **Set boundaries:** While offering support, it's important to set healthy boundaries. You can't solve all their problems, but you can offer a listening ear and encourage them to seek professional help if needed.

- **Respect their privacy:** Don't pressure them to share more than they're comfortable with. Let them know the conversation is confidential unless they express thoughts of harming themselves or others.

- **Be patient:** Building trust and creating a space for open communication takes time. Don't get discouraged if they're not ready to talk right away.

By following these tips and starting open conversations about mental health, we can create a more supportive world where individuals feel empowered to seek help and find healing.

Addressing Stigma and Promoting Understanding

The stigma surrounding mental health is a significant barrier to seeking help and obtaining treatment. This stigma can manifest as negative attitudes, beliefs, and stereotypes that create feelings of shame, isolation, and fear of judgment. In this section, we'll explore ways to address stigma and promote understanding.

The Effects of Stigma:

- **Prevents People from Seeking Help:** Fear of being judged or ostracized can prevent individuals from acknowledging their struggles and reaching out for professional help. This can delay treatment and worsen mental health outcomes.

- **Creates Feelings of Shame and Isolation:** Stigma can make individuals feel ashamed of their mental health condition, leading to social isolation and a sense of being alone in their struggles.

- **Hinders Open Communication:** The fear of stigma can create an environment where individuals are hesitant to talk openly about mental health, perpetuating the cycle of misunderstanding.

Combating Stigma:

- **Education is Key:** The more we understand about mental health conditions, the less likely we are to hold onto negative stereotypes. Educate yourself and others about the realities of mental health – the causes, symptoms, and available treatment options.

- **Challenge Misconceptions:** Don't hesitate to correct misconceptions about mental health when you hear them. Explain that mental health conditions are treatable and not a sign of weakness.

- **Share your Story:** If you're comfortable doing so, sharing your own experiences with mental health can be a powerful tool for promoting understanding. It can normalize the conversation and show others they're not alone.

- **Challenge Sexist and Racist Biases:** Recognize that mental health conditions can affect people of all backgrounds. Be mindful of cultural biases that might contribute to stigma within certain communities.

- **Promote Positive Representation:** Support media portrayals that depict mental health conditions realistically and highlight the importance of seeking help.

- **Focus on Empathy:** Approach conversations about mental health with compassion and understanding. Remember that people with mental health conditions are individuals just like you, deserving of respect and support.

- **Use Inclusive Language:** Avoid language that stigmatizes mental health conditions. Instead of saying someone is "crazy" or "psychotic," use respectful terms like "someone living with a mental health condition."

- **Be a Role Model:** Promote open and honest conversations about mental health in your own social circles. By leading by example, you can encourage others to do the same.

By working together to address stigma and promote understanding, we can create a world where mental health struggles are met with empathy and support, not judgment. Everyone deserves to feel comfortable seeking help and on the path to healing.

Building a Support Network and Community Resources

No one should face mental health challenges alone. Building a strong support network and utilizing available community resources are essential for walk through the difficult times and promoting overall well-being. This section will equip you with strategies for building a network of support and accessing helpful resources.

The Benefits of a Support Network:

- **Reduced Isolation:** Knowing you have people who care about you and understand your struggles can alleviate feelings of isolation and loneliness.

- **Increased Emotional Support:** A support network can provide a safe space to share your feelings, vent frustrations, and receive encouragement.

- **Practical Help:** Supportive friends, family members, or therapists can offer practical help with daily tasks when you're struggling. This can include things like running errands, preparing meals, or offering childcare.

- **Enhanced Sense of Control:** Having a support system can empower you and give you a sense of control over your situation.

Building Your Support Network:

- **Reach out to Loved Ones:** Talk to trusted friends, family members, or partners about your mental health challenges. Let them know what kind of support you need, whether it's a listening ear, someone to accompany you to a therapy appointment, or help with daily tasks.

- **Join a Support Group:** Connecting with others who share similar experiences can be incredibly validating and provide a sense of belonging. Support groups can be found online or in your local community.

- **Seek Professional Help:** Therapists and counselors can provide expert guidance, support, and evidence-based treatment for mental health conditions.

Utilizing Community Resources:

- **Mental Health Hotlines:** These resources offer immediate support and crisis intervention for those experiencing emotional distress.

- **Mental Health Awareness Websites:** Many reputable websites offer reliable information about mental health conditions, treatment options, and available resources.

- **Community Mental Health Centers:** These facilities often provide affordable or free therapy services, support groups, and medication management.

- **Employee Assistance Programs (EAPs):** Many workplaces offer confidential counseling services and resources for employees experiencing mental health challenges.

Things to consider:

- **Don't be afraid to ask for help:** Building a support network is not a sign of weakness. Everyone needs help sometimes.

- **Consider different forms of support:** Your support network doesn't have to be limited to friends and family. Therapists, support groups, and online resources can also be valuable sources of support.

- **The needs of your support network may change:** As your situation changes, your needs for support may evolve. Communicate openly with your support network about your changing needs.

By building a strong support network and utilizing available community resources, you can create a circle of strength around yourself. Knowing you're not alone and having access to help can make a significant difference in your journey towards mental well-being.

A Guide to Supporting Someone With Mental Health Issues

Seeing someone you care about struggle with mental health can feel overwhelming. You might wonder how to best approach them, what to say, or how much help you can realistically offer. The truth is that even small gestures of support can make a significant difference. This guide explores ways to create a safe space, offer meaningful support, and encourage professional help for someone you love who is battling mental health challenges.

Creating a Safe Space for Open Communication

One of the most crucial steps is fostering an environment where your loved one feels comfortable talking about their struggles. Here's how:

- **Active Listening:** Pay close attention, both verbally and nonverbally. Make eye contact, avoid interrupting, and offer encouraging nods to show you're engaged. Dr. Jade Wu, a clinical psychologist, emphasizes the importance of active listening. When someone opens up about their mental health, they're not looking for solutions or advice. They simply want to be heard and understood.

- **Non-judgmental Environment:** Avoid criticizing their feelings or experiences. Phrases like "You shouldn't feel that way" or "Everyone has problems, just get over it" can shut down communication. Instead, validate their emotions with empathy. "That sounds really difficult," or "I can't imagine how you must be feeling" can open the door to deeper conversation.

Sometimes, simply being present and offering a listening ear is the most powerful support you can give.

Offering Support Because Words and Actions Matter

Once you've created a safe space, here are ways to offer meaningful support:

- **Empathy and Encouragement:** Put yourself in their shoes and try to understand their perspective. Express empathy with phrases like "I'm so sorry you're going through this" or "I can see how much this is affecting you." Offer encouragement by reminding them of their strengths and past successes. Let them know you believe in them and their ability to overcome challenges.

- **Offer Practical Help:** Sometimes, the biggest burden can be daily tasks. Ask if there are specific things you can do to lighten their load. This could be anything from grocery shopping or picking up their kids to cleaning their house or running errands.

- **Respect Their Boundaries:** Be understanding if they don't always feel like talking or engaging. Don't force conversations, but let them know you're always there for them when they're ready.

- **Prayer:** If your loved one is religious or spiritual, you can offer to pray for them. The act of prayer itself can be a source of comfort and hope.

Actions speak louder than words. Support them not just with words of encouragement but by following through with practical help and respecting their boundaries.

Encouraging Professional Help: It's a Sign of Strength

While your support is invaluable, there may come a point where professional help is necessary. Here's how to encourage it effectively:

- **Normalize Therapy:** Therapy is not a sign of weakness. Many successful people seek therapy to manage stress, improve coping mechanisms, and gain a better understanding of themselves.

- **Offer to Help Find Resources:** Research therapists in their area and offer to help them schedule an appointment. This can be a daunting task on their own, so removing that hurdle can be a big step forward.

- **Be Patient with the Process:** Finding the right therapist is a journey. Be patient with them as they explore different options. Sometimes, it takes a few tries before a good fit is found. Mental health recovery takes time, so offer unwavering support throughout the process.

Seeking professional help is a sign of strength and self-awareness. Encourage them to prioritize their well-being and offer support as they embark on their healing journey.

Additional Considerations

Here are some additional points to keep in mind when supporting someone with mental health issues:

- **Educate Yourself:** Learn more about common mental health conditions such as anxiety, depression, and PTSD. Understanding the symptoms can help you be more empathetic and supportive.

- **Take Care of Yourself:** Supporting someone with mental health challenges can be emotionally draining. Make sure to prioritize your own self-care to avoid burnout. This could involve activities like exercise, spending time in nature, or connecting with supportive friends and family.

You should keep in mind that mental health issues are real and can be debilitating. Approach your loved one with compassion and understanding. By creating a safe space, offering meaningful support, and encouraging professional help, you can make a significant difference in their journey towards healing.

Resources and Support Groups

While your support is vital, there are supplementary resources available to your loved one:

- **Support Groups:** Connecting with others who understand similar struggles can be incredibly helpful. Encourage them to research online support groups or local mental health organizations that offer peer-to-peer support.

- **Hotlines and Crisis Services:** In times of crisis, there are hotlines and crisis services available 24/7 to provide immediate support and intervention. Help them find the contact information for these services and keep it readily available.

- **Mental Health Apps and Online Resources:** There are many helpful apps and online resources that offer mental health exercises, coping mechanisms, and information on various conditions. Explore these options together and see if any resonate with them.

Another thing you should consider is that recovery is a journey, not a destination. There will be setbacks and challenges along the way. Be patient and understanding, and celebrate their victories, big or small.

The Power of Hope and Resilience

Mental health struggles can feel overwhelming, but with the right support and resources, recovery is absolutely possible. Here are some quotes that offer hope and inspiration:

- "The bravest thing we can do sometimes is just to show up." - Brené Brown

- "You don't have to be okay all the time. The world isn't always okay." - Holley Gerth

- "One day or day one. You decide." - Jackie Thompson

Your love and support can be a powerful source of strength for your loved one. Encourage them to hold onto hope and believe in their resilience. They are not alone in this battle, and with the right support system, they can overcome their challenges and thrive.

Taking the First Step:

If you're unsure where to start, here are some resources to get you on the right track:

- The National Alliance on Mental Illness (NAMI)

- MentalHealth.gov

- The Jed Foundation

By taking the first step to educate yourself, create a safe space, and offer support, you can make a world of difference in the life of someone struggling with mental health challenges. Remember, you are not alone in this journey.

Conclusion

Supporting someone with mental health issues is a process that involves love, patience, and unwavering encouragement. While it may seem challenging at times, remember that even the smallest gestures can have a profound impact. By creating a safe space for open communication, offering practical and emotional support, and encouraging professional help when needed, you become a beacon of hope in their darkest moments.

If you want spiritual guidance, then the Bible offers a wealth of comfort and inspiration for those struggling with mental health challenges. Psalms 46:1 assures us, "God is our refuge and strength, an ever-present help in trouble." When your loved one feels lost and alone, remind them of God's constant presence and unwavering love. Philippians 4:13 offers further encouragement: "I can do all things through him who strengthens me." Even when they feel weak and incapable, God's strength can carry them through.

This process of mental well-being may not be easy but know that you are not alone. There are resources available, and support groups exist to offer a sense of community and understanding. Most importantly, have faith in the power of hope and resilience. With continuous support, professional guidance, and a strong belief in their own strength, your loved one can overcome these challenges and experience a fulfilling life.

So, take that first step. Educate yourself, create a safe space, and extend your love and support. Your actions, combined with professional help and deep faith, can be the light that guides them on their path to healing. And most importantly, remember that you are a source of strength, and together, you can walk alongside them in hope.

Chapter 4:
Building Resilience

The human spirit is an extraordinary thing. It possesses an innate capacity for resilience, the ability to bounce back from adversity and emerge stronger. Throughout history, all cultures know that resilience is a necessary tool for living in a world often filled with hardship and prejudice.

In Chinese culture, Confucius highlighted the importance of resilience with his words, "Our greatest glory is not in never falling, but in rising every time we fall." This emphasizes that true success lies in the ability to recover and keep moving forward despite failures.

From Indian culture, Mahatma Gandhi famously said, "Strength does not come from physical capacity. It comes from an indomitable will." This underscores the idea that resilience is rooted in one's inner strength and determination, not just physical prowess.

Winston Churchill, the British Prime Minister during World War II, encouraged perseverance through his quote, "If you're going through hell, keep going." His words inspire us to continue pushing forward even in the most difficult times.

Helen Keller, who overcame immense personal challenges, stated, "Although the world is full of suffering, it is also full of the overcoming of it." Her perspective highlights the constant presence of both hardship and the ability to overcome it.

Finally, Nelson Mandela, reflecting on his struggle against apartheid in South Africa, said, "The greatest glory in living lies not in never falling, but in rising every time we fall." His experience and resilience remind us that the true measure of greatness is the ability to rise after setbacks.

Moving further, the Bible also talks about building resilience:

(Romans 5:3-5 (NIV):

- **"Not only so, but we also glory in our sufferings because we know that suffering produces perseverance; perseverance, character; and character, hope. And hope does not put us to shame because God's love has been poured out into our hearts through the Holy Spirit, who has been given to us."**

This verse reminds us that setbacks are inevitable, but it is through these challenges that we develop strength and rise again.

This chapter looks into the practicalities of building resilience. We'll explore various strategies, from cultivating mindfulness and relaxation techniques to overcoming fear and despair through spiritual practices. We'll also examine the importance of finding purpose and meaning in life, and the invaluable role a supportive community plays in bolstering resilience. So, whether you're facing a personal challenge or simply seeking to strengthen your inner core, this chapter provides a roadmap for building resilience and thriving in the face of adversity.

Strategies for Building Resilience and Coping Skills

Life is an unpredictable expedition, filled with both sunshine and storms. Building resilience equips us to weather the storms and emerge stronger. Here are some key strategies to cultivate resilience and develop effective coping skills:

- **Mindfulness and Relaxation Techniques:** The constant busyness of modern life can take a toll on our mental and emotional well-being. Learning to quiet the mind and cultivate inner peace is crucial for building resilience. Practices like meditation, deep breathing exercises, and spending time in nature can be powerful tools for managing stress and promoting relaxation.

- **Cognitive Restructuring:** Our thoughts significantly influence our emotions and behaviors. Negative self-talk and catastrophizing can exacerbate challenges. Cognitive restructuring teaches us to identify and challenge these unhelpful thought patterns. By reframing negative thoughts into more positive and realistic ones, we can improve our emotional well-being and build resilience.

- **Developing Problem-Solving Skills:** Life throws curveballs, and being able to navigate challenges effectively is a key aspect of resilience. Learning to break down problems into manageable steps, exploring different solutions, and developing a growth mindset (believing our abilities can improve) empowers us to overcome obstacles with confidence.

- **Building a Support Network:** No one is an island. Having a strong support network of friends, family, and loved ones provides a sense of belonging, encouragement, and practical assistance during difficult times. Connecting with a faith-based community or support groups can also offer invaluable social connections and shared experiences.

These are just a few examples, and the most effective strategies will vary depending on the individual. The key is to experiment, find what works best for you, and build a personalized toolkit for navigating life's challenges with resilience.

Mindful Living and Relaxation Techniques

In today's fast-paced world, our minds are constantly bombarded with stimuli. This constant busyness can make it difficult to manage stress and build resilience. Mindful living and relaxation techniques offer a powerful antidote to this constant mental chatter. By cultivating inner peace and present-moment awareness, we can develop the emotional strength to navigate life's challenges with greater ease.

Here are some specific strategies for incorporating mindful living and relaxation techniques into your daily routine:

- **Mindfulness Meditation:** Meditation is the practice of focusing your attention on the present moment without judgment. There are many different meditation techniques, but a simple practice involves sitting comfortably, closing your eyes, and focusing on your breath. Notice the sensation of your breath entering and leaving your nostrils. When your mind wanders (and it will!), gently guide your attention back to your breath. Start with short meditation sessions (5-10 minutes) and gradually increase the duration as you become more comfortable.

- **Deep Breathing Exercises:** Deep, slow breathing activates the body's relaxation response, counteracting the stress response triggered by fight-or-flight situations. There are various deep breathing techniques, but a simple method involves inhaling slowly through your nose for a count of four, holding your breath for a count of two, and exhaling slowly through your mouth for a count of six. Repeat this cycle for several minutes, focusing on the sensation of your chest and abdomen rising and falling.

- **Progressive Muscle Relaxation:** This technique involves tensing and relaxing different muscle groups in your body. By focusing on the contrasting sensations of tension and relaxation, you can release built-up stress throughout your body. Begin by tensing your toes for a few seconds, then releasing and focusing on the feeling of relaxation. Repeat this process with each major muscle group, working your way up your body.

- **Mindful Movement:** Movement can be a powerful tool for managing stress and promoting relaxation. Activities like yoga, tai chi, and gentle walking can help you connect with your body and cultivate present-moment awareness. Focus on the sensations of your breath and body as you move rather than getting caught up in thoughts about the past or future.

- **Spending Time in Nature:** Immersing yourself in nature has a well-documented calming effect on the mind and body. Studies show that spending time outdoors can reduce stress hormones, improve mood, and boost creativity. Take a walk in the park, sit by a stream, or simply gaze at the stars. Connecting with nature allows you to step outside the constant busyness of your mind and find a sense of peace and perspective.

Remember, building a mindful practice takes time and consistency. Be patient with yourself and celebrate small victories. By incorporating these techniques into your daily routine, you'll cultivate inner peace, enhance your resilience, and create a solid foundation for navigating life's challenges with greater ease.

Overcoming Fear, Doubt, and Despair Through Spiritual Practices

Fear, doubt, and despair are powerful emotions that can challenge our resilience and leave us feeling lost. Spiritual practices, rooted in Biblical truths and spiritual disciplines, offer a wellspring of strength and hope to navigate these dark waters. For many, faith has been a cornerstone of resilience, providing solace, guidance, and a sense of purpose even in the face of immense hardship. Here's how these practices can help us overcome fear, doubt, and despair:

- **Connection to Something Greater:** Spiritual practices often connect us to a force or being larger than ourselves. This connection fosters a sense of belonging and purpose, reminding us that we are not alone in our struggles. The Bible teaches that we are part of a greater plan, as seen in Jeremiah 29:11: "For I know the plans I have for you," declares the Lord, "plans to prosper you and not to harm you, plans to give you hope and a future." This assurance can be a powerful anchor during times of fear and doubt.

- **Finding Meaning and Purpose:** Reflecting on the deeper meaning of life and our place in the universe is encouraged through spiritual practices. Discovering purpose, whether it's serving others, contributing to a larger cause, or living a life of love and compassion, can provide a sense of direction and motivation. Romans 8:28 reminds us, "And we know that in all things God works for the good of those who love him, who have been called according to his purpose." This belief can help us find strength and purpose even when faced with challenges.

- **Seeking Forgiveness and Letting Go:** Fear and doubt can often be rooted in past hurts and unresolved issues. Jesus emphasize the importance of forgiveness, both for ourselves and others. Ephesians 4:32 advises, "Be kind and compassionate to one another, forgiving each other, just as in Christ God forgave you." By letting go of anger and resentment, we free ourselves from the shackles of the past and move forward with a lighter heart.

- **Prayer and Meditation:** Prayer and meditation are powerful tools for cultivating inner peace and fostering a sense of connection to the divine. Through prayer, we express our vulnerabilities, anxieties, and hopes to a higher power. Philippians 4:6-7 encourages us, "Do not be anxious about anything, but in every situation, by prayer and petition, with thanksgiving, present your requests to God. And the peace of God, which transcends all understanding, will guard your hearts and your minds in Christ Jesus." Meditation allows us to quiet the mind and access a deeper wellspring of strength and resilience within ourselves.

- **Community and Support:** Many religious traditions offer a strong sense of community, providing a network of support and encouragement during difficult times. Surrounding yourself with like-minded individuals who share your values and beliefs can be a powerful source of strength and comfort. Hebrews 10:24-25 highlights this, "And let us consider how we may spur one another on toward love and good deeds, not giving up meeting together, as some are in the habit of doing, but encouraging one another—and all the more as you see the Day approaching."

It's important to note that spiritual practices can take many forms. Finding a path that resonates with your beliefs and values is key. Whether it's attending religious services, spending time in nature, or practicing daily affirmations of gratitude, cultivating a sense of connection, meaning, and hope in your life is essential. By doing so, you'll equip yourself with the inner strength to overcome fear, doubt, and despair and build a life of resilience and joy guided by spiritual disciplines and Biblical truths.

Finding Purpose, Meaning, and Hope in God's Plan for Our Lives

Life can be a whirlwind of challenges and uncertainties. During these times, we often grapple with questions of purpose and meaning. For many who find solace in faith, the belief in God's plan for our lives offers a powerful source of strength and hope. The Bible is full of verses that remind us of God's love and His desire for our well-being:

- **Jeremiah 29:11:** "For I know the plans I have for you," declares the Lord, "plans to prosper you and not to harm you, plans to give you hope and a future." (NIV) This verse assures us that God has a purpose for each of us, even when we can't see it ourselves. His plan is not to harm us but to bring us good and a future filled with hope.

- **Romans 8:28:** "And we know that in all things God works for the good of those who love him, who have been called according to his purpose." (NIV) This verse offers comfort in the midst of hardship. It reminds us that even during difficult times, God is working in our lives, shaping us and drawing us closer to Him. His purpose for us, ultimately, is good.

Finding Your Purpose:

So, how do we discover God's plan for our lives? Here are some ways to explore this question:

- **Prayer:** Prayer is a powerful tool for communication with God. Through prayer, we can express our desires, anxieties, and hopes. As we open ourselves to God, He can guide us and reveal His purpose for our lives.

- **Reflection and Journaling:** Taking time for quiet reflection allows us to connect with our inner selves and what truly matters to us. Journaling can be a helpful tool for exploring your values, strengths, and passions. By reflecting on these aspects, you might discover areas where your gifts and talents can be used to serve God and others.

- **Serving Others:** One of the most fulfilling ways to connect with God's purpose is by serving others. Look for opportunities to volunteer in your community or church. Helping those in need can be a powerful way to experience God's love and discover your unique purpose in His plan.

- **Reading Scripture:** The Bible is filled with stories of people who found their purpose in God. Reading these stories can offer inspiration and guidance. Pay attention to verses that resonate with your heart and offer insight into your strengths and calling.

However, keep in mind that the process of discovering God's plan for your life is an ongoing process. There will be times of clarity and confusion. Trust in God's love and guidance, and be open to the opportunities He presents along the way. As you walk in faith, you'll gain a deeper understanding of your purpose and experience the hope and strength that come from knowing you are part of something bigger than yourself.

The Strength of Connection

No one thrives in isolation. Building a strong support network is a cornerstone of resilience. This network can come in many forms, each offering unique benefits:

- **Church Community:** For many people of faith, the church provides a vital source of support and connection. Surrounding yourself with like-minded individuals who share your values and beliefs fosters a sense of belonging and acceptance. Participating in church activities, volunteering, or simply attending services can offer opportunities for social interaction, encouragement, and spiritual growth.

- **Family and Friends:** Strong bonds with family and friends provide emotional support, practical assistance, and a sense of belonging. Sharing your challenges and triumphs with loved ones can lighten your load and offer a sense of perspective. Nurture these relationships by investing time and energy into them.

- **Support Groups:** Connecting with others who share similar challenges can be incredibly empowering. Support groups offer a safe space to share experiences, learn coping mechanisms, and gain encouragement from others who understand what you're going through. There are support groups available for a wide range of mental health challenges, as well as for specific demographics or faith-based communities.

- **Shared Interests:** Engaging in activities you enjoy can be a powerful way to connect with others who share your passions. This could involve joining a sports team, a book club, or an art class. Having shared interests provides a sense of community, reduces stress, and offers opportunities for social interaction and positive reinforcement.

Building Your Support Network:

Here are some tips for building a strong support network:

- **Be Open and Honest:** Building genuine connections requires vulnerability. Be open about your struggles and challenges. The right people will offer support and understanding, not judgment.

- **Be a Good Friend:** Strong support networks are a two-way street. Be there for your loved ones when they need you. Offer a listening ear, practical help, or simply a shoulder to cry on.

- **Set Boundaries:** While connection is important, it's also crucial to set healthy boundaries. Don't overload yourself by taking on more than you can handle. Communicate your needs clearly and prioritize your well-being.

- **Be Patient:** Building a strong support network takes time and effort. Don't get discouraged if it doesn't happen overnight. Be patient, keep putting yourself out there, and nurture the connections you make.

A strong support network acts as a safety net, catching you when you fall and offering the strength and encouragement you need to get back up. By cultivating connections with your church community, family, friends, and those who share your interests, you build a powerful foundation for resilience and confront life's challenges with greater ease.

Conclusion

Building resilience is a process that requires a multifaceted approach. It involves cultivating inner strength, developing coping skills, and creating a strong support network. As the renowned writer and activist James Baldwin once said, "Not everything that is faced can be changed, but nothing can be changed until it is faced." This powerful statement summarizes the essence of resilience – the courage to confront challenges head-on and the determination to emerge stronger on the other side.

The Bible also offers profound wisdom on this topic. In 2 Corinthians 12:10, we read, "For when I am weak, then I am strong." This paradoxical truth reminds us that our greatest strength can emerge from our greatest vulnerabilities. By embracing our challenges and seeking support, we can tap into a reservoir of inner power.

Remember, resilience is not about being invincible; it's about finding the strength to persevere through adversity. By incorporating mindfulness, spiritual practices, and strong connections into your life, you're building a foundation for resilience that will serve you well in every aspect of your life. Take the first step, celebrate your progress, and never underestimate the power of your own spirit.

As Maya Angelou wisely observed, "I've learned that people will forget what you said, people will forget what you did, but people will never forget how you made them feel." By building resilience and supporting others, you create a ripple effect of positivity that extends far beyond yourself.

Chapter 5:
Seeking Professional Help

Mental health, like physical health, requires care and attention. While resilience, support systems, and spiritual practices are invaluable, there are times when professional help is essential. As the renowned psychiatrist Carl Jung stated, "The unconscious is the unknown in the soul, and the greatest part of the soul is unknown." Seeking professional help can illuminate the hidden corners of our minds and hearts, offering insights and tools for healing.

The Bible also acknowledges the complexities of the human psyche. In Proverbs 16:32, we find, "Whoever is slow to anger has great understanding, but he who has a hasty temper exalts folly." This verse recognizes that our emotions and behaviors are interconnected (Proverbs 1:5 "A wise man will listen and increase his learning, and a discerning man will obtain guidance").

This chapter will explore the importance of professional diagnosis and treatment, exploring the roles of pastors, counselors, and therapists in holistic healing. We will also provide practical steps for seeking mental health support and highlight available resources. By understanding the benefits of professional help and overcoming the stigma surrounding mental health, we can empower ourselves and others to seek the support needed for optimal well-being.

Importance of Professional Diagnosis and Treatment

The decision to seek professional help for mental health concerns is a significant step. It often involves overcoming stigma, fear, and uncertainty. However, it's crucial to understand that professional diagnosis and treatment are essential components of holistic well-being.

A professional mental health provider brings specialized knowledge and expertise to the table. They are trained to assess symptoms, conduct thorough evaluations, and accurately diagnose mental health conditions. This process is vital for developing an effective treatment plan. As argued by many authors, the process of recovery is not a matter of willpower alone. It involves learning new skills, developing new coping mechanisms, and challenging old beliefs.

A correct diagnosis is the cornerstone of effective treatment. It helps individuals understand their condition, manage expectations, and seek appropriate interventions. Without a proper diagnosis, individuals may receive ineffective or even harmful treatments. Moreover, a professional can differentiate between various mental health conditions, ensuring that the right treatment is administered.

Treatment, whether through therapy, medication, or a combination of both, is guided by the diagnosis. It addresses the underlying causes of symptoms and provides strategies for managing them. Professional guidance is essential in navigating the complexities of mental health, as it offers support, accountability, and evidence-based interventions.

Incorporating evidence-based practices, professionals stay updated on the latest research and treatment modalities. They can offer personalized recommendations based on individual needs and circumstances. This ensures that individuals receive the most effective and up-to-date care.

It's important to note that while many people find solace in faith and support systems, these alone may not be sufficient for addressing complex mental health issues. Professional treatment complements spiritual and communal support, offering a comprehensive approach to healing. As the renowned psychiatrist Viktor Frankl stated, "Between stimulus and response, there is a space. In that space is our power to choose our response. In that choice lies our growth and our freedom." With professional guidance, individuals can develop the tools to navigate that space effectively and make choices that promote healing and growth.

Therefore, seeking professional diagnosis and treatment is a proactive step towards improved mental health. It provides access to expert knowledge, evidence-based interventions, and personalized care. By prioritizing professional help, individuals can take a first step towards healing and recovery, ultimately leading to a more fulfilling and resilient life.

Understanding the Role of Pastors, Counselors, and Therapists in Holistic Healing

Holistic healing encompasses the interconnectedness of mind, body, and spirit. In addressing mental health, a multidisciplinary approach often yields the most effective results. Pastors, counselors, and therapists each bring unique perspectives and expertise to the table, contributing to a comprehensive healing process.

The Role of Pastors

Pastors, as spiritual leaders, offer a vital role in the holistic healing journey. They provide spiritual guidance, support, and a sense of community. Their role often includes:

- **Spiritual Counseling:** Pastors offer spiritual counsel, drawing on religious teachings and practices to address emotional and spiritual concerns. They help individuals find meaning and purpose in their struggles.

- **Prayer and Intercession:** Prayer is a cornerstone of pastoral care. Pastors offer prayers for individuals seeking healing and guidance, connecting them to a higher power.

- **Community Building:** Pastors foster a supportive community where individuals can find belonging and encouragement. This sense of connection can be instrumental in the healing process.

The Role of Counselors

Counselors are mental health professionals trained in various therapeutic approaches. They focus on the psychological and emotional aspects of well-being. Their role typically involves:

- **Psychotherapy:** Counselors provide therapeutic interventions to help individuals understand and manage their emotions, thoughts, and behaviors. They offer tools for coping with stress, anxiety, depression, and other mental health challenges.

- **Problem-Solving:** Counselors assist individuals in developing problem-solving skills and making informed decisions. They help clients identify and overcome obstacles in their lives.

- **Relationship Counseling:** Counselors can help individuals improve their relationships with partners, family members, and friends. They offer guidance on communication, conflict resolution, and building healthy connections.

The Role of Therapists

Therapists, a broader term encompassing various mental health professionals, provide specialized care for a range of mental health conditions. Their role often includes:

- **Diagnosis:** Therapists conduct comprehensive assessments to identify underlying mental health conditions. This accurate diagnosis is crucial for developing an effective treatment plan.

- **Medication Management:** Psychiatrists, a type of therapist, prescribe and manage medications to treat mental health conditions. They work closely with other mental health professionals to ensure optimal care.

- **Specialized Treatment:** Different therapists offer specialized treatments, such as cognitive-behavioral therapy (CBT), dialectical behavior therapy (DBT), or psychodynamic therapy. These approaches target specific symptoms and underlying issues.

It's essential to recognize that these roles are not mutually exclusive. Many pastors incorporate counseling techniques into their ministry, and some counselors may also offer spiritual guidance. The most effective approach often involves collaboration between these professionals to provide comprehensive care.

By understanding the unique contributions of pastors, counselors, and therapists, individuals can make informed decisions about seeking the support they need. A holistic approach that addresses the spiritual, psychological, and emotional dimensions of well-being is crucial for achieving lasting healing and resilience.

Steps to Take When Seeking Mental Health Support

Seeking mental health support can feel overwhelming, but taking proactive steps can make the process smoother and more effective. Here's a detailed guide to help you walk through this important process:

1. Self-Assessment

Recognize the Signs:

- Pay close attention to your emotions and behaviors. Persistent sadness, anxiety, changes in sleep or appetite, and difficulty concentrating are key indicators. As Confucius said, "The journey of a thousand miles begins with a single step." Recognizing these signs is that crucial first step.

Prioritize Your Well-being:

- Understand that seeking help is a sign of strength, not weakness. It takes courage to acknowledge when you need support. Remember, "You, yourself, as much as anybody in the entire universe, deserve your love and affection," as Buddha wisely noted.

2. Research Available Resources

Identify Local Providers:

- Research mental health professionals in your area. Look into their insurance coverage, areas of expertise, and treatment modalities. Consider the words of Viktor Frankl: "When we are no longer able to change a situation, we are challenged to change ourselves." Finding the right provider is a step towards that change.

Explore Online Resources:

- Utilize online platforms to find therapists or counselors. Many offer detailed profiles, reviews, and appointment scheduling options. The digital age has brought mental health support to our fingertips, making it easier to find the right match for your needs.

Consider Support Groups:

- Explore support groups that align with your specific concerns. These groups offer peer support and practical coping strategies. Helen Keller said, "Alone we can do so little; together we can do so much." Support groups embody this principle, providing collective strength.

3. Reach Out to a Trusted Individual

Share Your Feelings:

- Talk to a friend, family member, or trusted confidant about your decision to seek help. Their support can be invaluable. As Mr. Rogers reminded us, "Anything that's human is mentionable, and anything that is mentionable can be more manageable."

Consider a Support Person:

- Having someone accompany you to appointments can provide comfort and reassurance. This trusted individual can help you remember important details and offer emotional support.

4. Initial Contact

Contact a Mental Health Professional:

- Reach out to a therapist, counselor, or psychiatrist to schedule an initial appointment. Initiating this contact can feel daunting, but it's a significant step forward.

Be Honest and Open:

- During the initial consultation, be candid about your symptoms, concerns, and treatment goals. Honesty helps professionals tailor their approach to your needs. Carl Rogers emphasized the importance of authenticity: "The curious paradox is that when I accept myself just as I am, then I can change."

5. Treatment Plan

Collaborate with Your Provider:

- Develop a comprehensive treatment plan that addresses your specific needs. This may involve therapy, medication, or a combination of both. Remember Gandhi's wisdom: "The best way to find yourself is to lose yourself in the service of others." Collaborating with your provider is a service to your future self.

Set Realistic Goals:

- Establish achievable goals for your mental health journey. Celebrate small victories to maintain motivation and track progress. "Success is the sum of small efforts, repeated day in and day out," as Robert Collier observed.

Be Patient:

- Healing takes time. Be patient with yourself and the process, understanding that progress may be gradual. The Taoist philosopher Lao Tzu said, "Nature does not hurry, yet everything is accomplished."

6. Utilize Available Resources

Take Advantage of Support Systems:

- Lean on your support network for encouragement and practical assistance. Friends and family can provide a safety net. "We rise by lifting others," said Robert Ingersoll. Your support system can help lift you up during challenging times.

Explore Complementary Therapies:

- Consider incorporating therapies like yoga, meditation, or acupuncture into your treatment plan. These can complement traditional treatments and enhance well-being. As the Dalai Lama stated, "Calm mind brings inner strength and self-confidence, so that's very important for good health."

Seek Educational Resources:

- Educate yourself about mental health conditions and treatment options. Knowledge empowers you to make informed decisions about your care. Francis Bacon famously said, "Knowledge is power." Use this power to navigate your mental health journey.

7. Self-Care

Prioritize Self-Care:

- Engage in activities that promote relaxation and well-being, such as exercise, hobbies, and spending time in nature. Thich Nhat Hanh taught, "To be beautiful means to be yourself. You don't need to be accepted by others. You need to accept yourself."

Manage Stress:

- Develop healthy coping mechanisms for managing stress. Techniques like deep breathing, mindfulness, or journaling can be helpful. "It's not stress that kills us, it is our reaction to it," said Hans Selye. Managing stress is about finding balance.

Get Enough Sleep:

- Aim for 7-9 hours of quality sleep each night. Good sleep is crucial for mental health and overall well-being. "A good laugh and a long sleep are the two best cures for anything," says an Irish proverb.

It is a true that seeking mental health support is a courageous step towards improved well-being. Be patient with yourself, celebrate your progress, and don't hesitate to reach out for additional support if needed. Taking these steps can help you walk through the process effectively and lead you towards a healthier, happier life. As Nelson Mandela said, "It always seems impossible until it's done."

Conclusion

Seeking professional help for mental health is evidence to one's courage and commitment to well-being. It's a journey that requires strength, resilience, and a willingness to embrace change. By prioritizing your mental health, you're not only investing in your own well-being but also creating a positive impact on those around you.

Remember, the path to healing is unique for everyone. There's no one-size-fits-all approach. It's essential to find the right professionals and support systems that align with your needs and values. Be patient with yourself, celebrate small victories, and don't hesitate to seek additional help if needed.

As you move forward, you may encounter challenges and setbacks. However, with the right support and perseverance, you can overcome obstacles and achieve lasting well-being. Respect the process, trust in your ability to heal, and remember that you are not alone.

What I believe is that the greatest discovery of all time is that a person can change his future by merely changing his attitude.

By taking the first step towards seeking professional help, you're empowering yourself to rewrite your story and create a brighter future.

Chapter 6:
Maintaining Mental Wellness

Feeling good about yourself is as important as looking after your body. It's like having a garden - you need to nurture it to make it bloom.

Mental health also plays an important role in making you happy. However, achieving mental health is a lifelong process that requires consistent effort and self-care. But happiness is not something readymade. It comes from your own actions.

This chapter explores practical strategies for maintaining long-term mental well-being. We will look into the importance of self-care, stress management, and a balanced lifestyle.

Additionally, we will examine the role of spiritual practices and strong relationships in promoting resilience and overall mental health. By incorporating these principles into daily life, individuals can build a solid foundation for emotional well-being and confront life's challenges with greater ease and grace.

Long-term Strategies for Maintaining Mental Wellness

Maintaining mental wellness is not a one-time effort or a quick fix. It requires long-term strategies that align with an individual's evolving emotional, physical, and social needs. While immediate coping mechanisms like deep breathing or quick meditation may offer short-term relief from stress, sustaining mental wellness over the years demands a more robust, adaptable, and intentional plan.

1. Consistent Self-care and Routine:

One of the most essential long-term strategies for mental wellness is the creation of a structured routine that incorporates regular self-care. The importance of consistency in caring for one's mental health cannot be overstated. Self-care routines that involve adequate sleep, regular physical exercise, and nutritious eating habits provide a strong foundation for emotional stability.

Sleep, for instance, plays a pivotal role in mental health. Chronic sleep deprivation can exacerbate feelings of anxiety, depression, and stress, leading to cognitive difficulties and emotional instability. By prioritizing 7-9 hours of quality sleep each night, individuals ensure that their minds and body have the necessary time to rest and recover. Likewise, engaging in regular physical activity—whether it's a daily walk, yoga, or more intense forms of exercise—releases endorphins, the body's natural stress relievers, which can elevate mood and reduce anxiety over time.

Similarly, maintaining a well-balanced diet is critical for brain function. Studies have shown that certain nutrients, such as omega-3 fatty acids, folic acid, and magnesium, support mental health by boosting brain activity and improving mood. A diet rich in vegetables, fruits, whole grains, and lean proteins can make a significant difference in how individuals feel mentally and emotionally.

A well-rounded self-care routine also involves activities that nourish the soul and provide emotional relief. These could include hobbies, artistic expression, or simply spending time with loved ones. Engaging in activities that bring joy, relaxation, or creativity helps balance the often overwhelming demands of life. The key to long-term self-care is sustainability: finding practices that can be integrated into daily life and enjoyed over time.

2. Ongoing Emotional Awareness and Reflection:

Maintaining mental wellness requires ongoing emotional awareness. This means regularly checking in with oneself to assess emotional well-being, recognize shifting moods, and address any underlying issues before they become overwhelming. Keeping a mental health journal or practicing daily reflection are excellent ways to track emotional states over time and identify patterns that might suggest the onset of stress or mental fatigue.

Reflection allows individuals to explore their emotional triggers, examine their reactions, and understand the deeper causes behind their feelings. This level of self-awareness is essential for long-term mental wellness because it enables proactive decision-making. Instead of reacting to stressful situations, individuals who practice emotional awareness can develop thoughtful responses grounded in self-compassion and mindfulness.

3. Developing Emotional Resilience:

Emotional resilience is a key component of long-term mental wellness. It refers to the ability to bounce back from setbacks, cope with challenges, and recover from adversity. Resilience doesn't mean avoiding stress or difficulty; rather, it's the capacity to face challenges with a sense of perspective and maintain a positive outlook. Developing resilience takes time and practice, but it can be cultivated through several approaches.

One way to build resilience is by fostering a mindset of growth and adaptability. By viewing challenges as opportunities for personal growth, individuals can shift their perspectives and reduce feelings of helplessness or frustration. This "growth mindset" allows for continuous learning, even in difficult circumstances, and promotes a sense of agency.

Another method of building resilience is through problem-solving skills. Mental wellness is significantly impacted when individuals feel powerless in the face of challenges. Learning how to break problems into manageable steps, assess potential solutions, and take action reduces anxiety and fosters a sense of control. This problem-solving approach can be applied to both small daily stresses and more significant life challenges.

Lastly, resilience is strengthened by a strong sense of purpose. Research shows that individuals who feel connected to a sense of meaning or purpose are more resilient when faced with adversity. Whether this purpose comes from one's career, personal relationships, or community involvement, having a reason to persevere is a powerful motivator for maintaining mental health in the long term.

4. Social Connections and Support Systems:

Long-term mental wellness is deeply tied to the quality of social connections and support systems. Studies have repeatedly shown that individuals with strong social networks—whether through family, friends, or community groups—are less likely to experience mental health issues like depression or anxiety. Meaningful social connections provide emotional support, reduce feelings of isolation, and offer a buffer against stress.

Building and maintaining these relationships requires intentionality. Long-term mental wellness doesn't just come from having people around but from cultivating deep, trusting relationships where individuals feel seen, heard, and supported. For some, this might involve engaging in regular social activities or maintaining close contact with family members. For others, it might mean joining support groups or participating in community organizations that foster a sense of belonging.

In a more practical sense, it's also helpful to have different kinds of relationships—some people can offer emotional support, others provide practical advice, and some may be companions for fun and relaxation. Diversifying social support systems ensures that individuals have access to a range of resources when facing difficult times.

Incorporating Self-care Practices into Daily Life

Incorporating self-care practices into daily life is more than a luxury; it is an essential component of sustaining mental wellness. While the concept of self-care is often associated with relaxation activities like spa days or vacations, true self-care is about creating daily habits that nurture both the mind and body. These small, consistent actions help build resilience, improve emotional well-being, and foster a positive mental state over time. The key is to make self-care a non-negotiable part of one's routine, integrating it into daily life in a way that feels sustainable and fulfilling.

Self-care practices can be as varied as the people who practice them. What works for one person may not resonate with another, and the key to long-term success lies in discovering personalized strategies that align with individual preferences, needs, and lifestyles. The beauty of self-care is that it doesn't require massive time commitments or expensive interventions. Instead, it thrives on regularity, simplicity, and mindfulness.

1. Morning Rituals:

Starting the day with a self-care routine sets a positive tone and establishes a foundation for mental well-being. Morning rituals could include activities like meditation, journaling, or simply enjoying a cup of coffee in silence before the hustle of the day begins. These moments of intentional calm allow individuals to center themselves, reflect on their intentions, and mentally prepare for the day's challenges.

For example, a simple 10-minute morning meditation can be an effective practice for clearing the mind, reducing anxiety, and fostering a sense of gratitude. Meditation helps individuals cultivate mindfulness, a state in which they remain present and fully engaged in their surroundings. Over time, this mindful practice can lead to increased focus, emotional stability, and a reduction in stress.

Another morning ritual could involve journaling. Spending a few minutes writing down thoughts, goals, or feelings can help clear mental clutter, process emotions, and create clarity around intentions for the day. Some people prefer to use gratitude journaling as a tool for self-care, where they reflect on things for which they are thankful. This practice shifts focus away from stressors and highlights the positive aspects of life, boosting mood and fostering a sense of appreciation.

2. Movement and Physical Exercise:

Incorporating movement into daily life is one of the most effective forms of self-care. Regular physical activity not only enhances physical health but also supports mental wellness by releasing endorphins, improving mood, and reducing stress. It doesn't necessarily have to be an intense workout—simple, enjoyable forms of movement can have profound benefits when done consistently.

For instance, a brisk 30-minute walk in nature is an excellent way to combine physical exercise with the mental health benefits of fresh air and a change of environment. Studies show that being outdoors, especially in natural settings, can significantly reduce symptoms of anxiety and depression. For those who may not enjoy traditional workouts, incorporating activities like dancing, yoga, or swimming can be equally beneficial.

The key to long-term physical self-care is finding an activity that brings joy and can be easily integrated into daily life. Whether it's a morning jog, an evening yoga session, or a midday stretch break, making movement a regular part of the routine can enhance both physical energy and mental clarity.

3. Mindful Breaks Throughout the Day:

Incorporating short, mindful breaks throughout the day is an often overlooked but powerful self-care practice. In a world that values constant productivity, taking moments to pause and reset can seem counterintuitive, but these breaks are essential for maintaining long-term mental wellness.

One example of a mindful break is the practice of "deep breathing." This simple technique can be done anywhere and only takes a few minutes. By focusing on slow, deep breaths, individuals can calm their nervous system, reduce feelings of stress, and restore a sense of mental equilibrium. Deep breathing exercises are particularly helpful in stressful work environments or during moments of high tension.

Another effective break could be stepping away from screens and devices for a few minutes to stretch or simply observe the surroundings. A few minutes of mindful observation or "grounding" can help reduce mental fatigue, improve focus, and renew energy. These small pauses throughout the day serve as opportunities to recharge, refocus, and maintain a balanced emotional state.

4. Evening Wind-down Rituals:

The way individuals end their day is just as important as how they begin it. Evening rituals that promote relaxation and rest can enhance sleep quality and reduce stress, ultimately supporting long-term mental wellness. One common evening self-care practice is the establishment of a "technology-free" period before bedtime. This means shutting down phones, computers, and other screens at least an hour before sleep to avoid overstimulation that can interfere with restful sleep.

Other evening rituals might include reading, listening to calming music, taking a warm bath, or engaging in gentle stretches. These activities help signal to the brain that it's time to wind down, creating a sense of calm that fosters deeper, more restorative sleep. Over time, these practices can have a profound impact on mental clarity, energy levels, and emotional resilience.

Strategies for Managing Stress in the Long Run

While stress is an inevitable part of life, how individuals manage it plays a significant role in their long-term mental wellness. Left unchecked, chronic stress can lead to serious mental and physical health issues, such as anxiety, depression, high blood pressure, and heart disease. Developing proactive strategies for managing stress over the long term helps mitigate these risks and supports overall well-being.

Unlike short-term stress management techniques like taking a quick walk or practicing deep breathing, long-term strategies focus on lifestyle changes, and mindset shifts that build resilience and reduce stress on a deeper level. These strategies are not designed to eliminate stress entirely—such a goal is unrealistic—but rather to equip individuals with the tools they need to respond to stress in a healthier, more constructive way.

1. Setting Boundaries and Learning to Say No:

One of the most important strategies for managing long-term stress is learning how to set healthy boundaries. Many people experience chronic stress because they overextend themselves—taking on too many responsibilities, saying "yes" to requests they don't have the capacity to fulfill, or allowing others to encroach on their time and energy.

Setting clear boundaries, both in personal and professional settings, is an act of self-preservation. It involves knowing one's limits, communicating them effectively, and not feeling guilty about prioritizing mental health. For example, if work demands are overwhelming, setting boundaries might involve discussing workload with a supervisor and negotiating more manageable expectations. In personal relationships, it might mean being honest about time constraints and not committing to social events that feel draining.

Learning to say "no" is another critical aspect of boundary-setting. Many people struggle with this, fearing disappointment or conflict, but saying "no" when necessary is an essential skill for reducing long-term stress. By saying "no" to unnecessary obligations, individuals free up time and energy to focus on self-care, personal goals, and activities that bring joy.

2. Prioritizing Time Management and Organization:

Poor time management is a significant source of stress for many people. When tasks pile up and deadlines loom, it's easy to feel overwhelmed and anxious. A long-term strategy for reducing this type of stress is to develop strong time management and organizational skills. This involves not only planning and scheduling but also making realistic assessments of what can be accomplished in a given timeframe.

For example, individuals might adopt a time-blocking method, where specific blocks of time are dedicated to particular tasks throughout the day. This approach helps create structure, reduces procrastination, and allows for more focused work. Another time management strategy is breaking large tasks into smaller, more manageable steps, which makes them feel less daunting and reduces feelings of stress.

The organization also plays a role in managing long-term stress. A cluttered environment can contribute to feelings of chaos and overwhelm, so maintaining an organized workspace or home can lead to a clearer, more focused mind. Simple practices like decluttering, keeping a to-do list, or using a calendar app to track tasks can significantly reduce stress levels over time.

3. Practicing Mindfulness and Meditation:

Mindfulness and meditation are two powerful tools for managing long-term stress. Both practices encourage individuals to be present, accept their emotions without judgment, and reduce overthinking. Meditation, in particular, has been shown to lower cortisol levels (the body's primary stress hormone), decrease anxiety, and promote a greater sense of calm and well-being.

A long-term meditation practice doesn't require hours of daily commitment. Even 10 to 15 minutes a day can yield significant benefits over time. Whether through guided meditations, mindfulness exercises, or even breathing techniques, these practices help individuals become more aware of their thoughts, better manage their reactions to stressors, and cultivate a more relaxed, balanced mindset.

Mindfulness, on the other hand, can be practiced throughout the day. For example, during a stressful work meeting, instead of reacting impulsively to tension, an individual might pause, take a deep breath, and focus on staying present. This simple act of mindfulness helps break the cycle of stress and fosters a more measured response to challenging situations.

4. Seeking Professional Help When Needed:

While self-care and personal strategies are essential for long-term stress management, there are times when professional help is necessary. Seeking the guidance of a therapist, counselor, or mental health professional can provide individuals with tools and coping mechanisms they may not have access to on their own.

For example, Cognitive Behavioral Therapy (CBT) is a widely recognized therapeutic approach that helps individuals identify and challenge negative thought patterns that contribute to stress. With the help of a trained therapist, individuals can develop new perspectives and behaviors that reduce anxiety and increase emotional resilience.

Recognizing when it's time to seek professional support is crucial to long-term mental wellness. Professional help can offer valuable insights, support, and strategies for managing stress and addressing any underlying mental health issues. It's a proactive step toward maintaining mental wellness and ensuring that stress is managed effectively over the long term. Therapy can provide a safe space to explore personal challenges, develop coping mechanisms, and gain perspective on how to navigate stressors in a healthier way. Additionally, mental health professionals can assist in creating a personalized plan for stress management, offering techniques tailored to individual needs and circumstances. Embracing professional support demonstrates a commitment to one's mental health and can be instrumental in achieving lasting well-being and resilience.

Embracing a Balanced Lifestyle and Healthy Choices with Spiritual, Emotional, and Physical Self-Care

Embracing a balanced lifestyle and making healthy choices is essential for maintaining mental wellness over the long term. This holistic approach includes attention to spiritual, emotional, and physical self-care, all of which play a vital role in overall well-being.

Applying Biblical Principles for Managing Stress, Anxiety, and Negative Thoughts

Applying biblical principles can offer a strong foundation for managing stress, anxiety, and negative thoughts. Many people find comfort and guidance in religious teachings, which can provide practical strategies and a sense of purpose in times of difficulty.

Trust in God

Trusting in God is a central biblical principle that can alleviate anxiety and stress. The Bible encourages believers to place their trust in God's plan and providence. For instance, Philippians 4:6-7 advises, "Do not be anxious about anything, but in every situation, by prayer and petition, with thanksgiving, present your requests to God. And the peace of God, which transcends all understanding, will guard your hearts and your minds in Christ Jesus." This verse underscores the importance of prayer and surrendering worries to God, which can lead to inner peace and reduced anxiety.

Renewing the Mind

Renewing the mind through scripture is another powerful principle for managing negative thoughts. Romans 12:2 teaches, "Do not conform to the pattern of this world but be transformed by the renewing of your mind. Then you will be able to test and approve what God's will is—his good, pleasing, and perfect will." Regular meditation on biblical passages can help shift negative thinking patterns and foster a positive outlook. For example, focusing on scriptures that emphasize God's love and promises can provide encouragement and counteract feelings of despair or inadequacy.

Seeking Support and Community

The Bible also emphasizes the importance of seeking support from others. Proverbs 27:17 states, "As iron sharpens iron, so one person sharpens another." Engaging with a supportive faith community, whether through church groups or prayer circles, can offer encouragement and practical advice during stressful times. Sharing struggles with others and receiving prayer and support can help alleviate feelings of isolation and provide a sense of belonging.

Incorporating these biblical principles into daily life can enhance mental wellness and provide a strong spiritual foundation for managing stress and anxiety. By trusting in God, renewing the mind through scripture, and seeking support from the faith community, individuals can cultivate resilience and maintain a balanced approach to handling life's challenges.

Nurturing Relationships, Community Support, and Spiritual Growth

Building and maintaining nurturing relationships, seeking community support, and fostering spiritual growth are crucial components of long-term mental wellness. These elements help create a supportive network that can enhance emotional stability and personal growth.

Family

Family relationships can be a source of immense support and comfort. Positive family dynamics, characterized by open communication, mutual respect, and unconditional love, contribute significantly to mental well-being. Healthy family interactions can provide a sense of belonging and stability, which are essential for emotional health. For instance, regular family gatherings or shared activities can strengthen bonds and offer opportunities for meaningful connections.

However, it's also important to recognize when family relationships become toxic or detrimental to mental health. In such cases, setting boundaries and seeking external support, such as counseling, can help manage the impact of these relationships. Maintaining a balance between fostering positive family connections and addressing conflicts or negative dynamics is crucial for maintaining overall mental wellness.

Friends

Friendships play a vital role in emotional support and social engagement. Surrounding oneself with supportive and positive friends can enhance well-being by providing companionship, encouragement, and practical help. For example, friends who listen empathetically and offer constructive advice can be invaluable during challenging times.

On the other hand, it's important to evaluate the quality of friendships and their impact on your well-being. Friendships that are consistently negative or draining can contribute to stress and anxiety. Identifying and distancing oneself from such relationships while nurturing those that are uplifting and supportive is essential for maintaining a positive social environment. Regularly assessing and adjusting your social circle based on how individuals contribute to your mental health can help ensure that your friendships support rather than hinder your well-being.

Community

Engaging with a supportive community can provide a sense of belonging and purpose. Participating in community activities with like-minded individuals fosters connections and creates opportunities for personal growth and support. Whether through local clubs, volunteer organizations, or interest-based groups, being involved in community activities helps build a network of supportive relationships and contributes to a sense of fulfillment.

Finding a community that aligns with your interests and values can enhance mental wellness. For instance, joining a group that shares your hobbies or passions can provide emotional support and reduce feelings of isolation. Activities such as group fitness classes, book clubs, or charitable events can offer both social interaction and a sense of achievement.

Spiritual Growth

Spiritual growth is a key aspect of mental wellness, offering guidance and strength through life's challenges. Understanding and aligning with your church's values and teachings can deepen your spiritual connection and enhance your sense of purpose. For example, if your church emphasizes values such as compassion, forgiveness, and community service, engaging in these practices can reinforce your spiritual beliefs and support mental well-being.

Regular spiritual practices, such as attending church services, participating in study groups, and personal reflection, contribute to growth and resilience. Ensuring that your spiritual activities align with biblical teachings can provide a solid foundation for navigating stress and adversity. For instance, integrating prayer and meditation into your daily routine can foster a sense of peace and clarity.

Overall, nurturing relationships, seeking community support, and focusing on spiritual growth create a comprehensive support system for mental wellness. By investing in positive family interactions, cultivating supportive friendships, engaging in community activities, and aligning with spiritual values, individuals can build a robust framework for maintaining mental health and well-being.

To summarize, taking care of your mental wellness involves many parts of your life. It includes building strong relationships, having community support, and growing spiritually. Approach life with this belief that happiness is the meaning and purpose of life, the whole aim and end of human existence.

By focusing on self-care, making strong connections, and finding spiritual fulfillment, we can build a strong base for our well-being. It's not about being perfect but making progress. Small, consistent steps can make a big difference in mental health.

The Bible says in Proverbs 17:17, "A friend loves at all times, and a brother is born for adversity." Strong relationships are important, especially during tough times. They offer support and encouragement. By investing in our relationships and growing spiritually, we find resilience and hope.

And the process of mental wellness is personal. It takes self-awareness, self-compassion, and seeking support. By connecting mind, body, and spirit, we can live a life filled with purpose, joy, and fulfillment.

Lastly, you must believe that you are not alone. Seek support from loved ones, mental health professionals, or spiritual leaders when needed. Your well-being is important, and you deserve a full and healthy life.

Conclusion

This book has taken you through the many layers of mental health – peeling back the surface to reveal its deep importance while also offering practical steps to bring about real change in your life. From the gentle power of self-care to the profound impact of relationships and the quiet strength found in spirituality, each element has shown how connected your mental well-being is to everything else.

But here's the thing – caring for your mental health isn't a straight path, nor is it a finish line you cross. It's unpredictable, sometimes messy, and definitely not a one-size-fits-all kind of thing. It's about progress, not perfection. You might take a big leap one day and barely a step the next.

Yet, even those tiny, almost unnoticeable steps can lead to the most unexpected and remarkable changes. Imagine tending a garden – sometimes you see the flowers bloom, but other times, you're just watering the soil. As a sane person once said, "It is not how much you do, but how much you enjoy what you do that matters."

In this process, you might find yourself overwhelmed one day and hopeful the next. That's okay. There will be days when everything feels clear and others when the fog returns. But here's the beauty – it's during those confusing, heavy moments that you often discover your greatest strength. As Maya Angelou so perfectly put it, "Do the best you can until you know better. Then, when you know better, do better."

And remember, reaching out for help is not a weakness. It's an act of bravery. When you connect with others – whether it's family, friends, or professionals – you create a web of support that can catch you when you stumble. Because the truth is, we're not meant to do this alone. As the Dalai Lama reminds us, "Compassion for others begins with kindness to ourselves." You have to be kind to yourself first before you can truly find peace in your world.

Sometimes, when everything seems to be falling apart, it's actually falling into place in ways you can't yet see. Let the light in, even when it feels like shadows are all around. As Helen Keller said, "Keep your face to the sunshine, and you cannot see the shadow." Stay focused on that light, and even in the hardest moments, trust that it's leading you to something better.

Life doesn't wait for you to have everything figured out. And that's okay – you don't need to have all the answers. You just need to keep moving forward, one step at a time, with patience and grace for yourself. Even when you stumble, remember Leonard Cohen's words, "There is a crack in everything; that's how the light gets in." Those cracks don't make you weak – they make you human, and they let the light shine through even brighter.

Manufactured by Amazon.ca
Acheson, AB

14401701R00050